## 21st Century Skills Library

REAL WORLD SCIENCE

# PLANTS

*Elizabeth Silverthorne*

**Cherry Lake Publishing**
**Ann Arbor, Michigan**

Published in the United States of America by Cherry Lake Publishing
Ann Arbor, Michigan
www.cherrylakepublishing.com

Content Adviser: Laura Graceffa, middle school science teacher; BA degree in science, Vassar College; MA degrees in science and education, Brown University

Photo Credits: Cover and page 1, © Shutterstock; page 4, © Shutterstock; page 6, © Theo Gaitaneris/Shutterstock; page 7, © Sabino Parente/Shutterstock; page 10, © Clearviewstock/Shutterstock; page 12, © spfotocz/Shutterstock; page 13, © MilousSK/Shutterstock; page 15, © mdd/Shutterstock; page 16, © Craig Melville/Shutterstock; page 18, © Ervin Monn/Shutterstock; page 19, © Dole/Shutterstock; page 21, © Ly Dinh Quoc Vu/Shutterstock; page 22, © Anton Foltin/Shutterstock; page 24, © Gail Johnson/Shutterstock; page 26, © Gusev Mikhail Eugenievich / Shutterstock; page 28, © Mariusz S. Jurgielewicsz/Shutterstock

Library of Congress Cataloging-in-Publication Data

Silverthorne, Elizabeth, 1930-
Plants / Elizabeth Silverthorne.
    p. cm. — (Real world science)
ISBN-13: 978-1-60279-461-0
ISBN-10: 1-60279-461-8
1. Botany—Juvenile literature.  I. Title. II. Series.

QK49.S55 2009
580—dc22                                                    2008040805

Cherry Lake Publishing would like to acknowledge the work of
The Partnership for 21st Century Skills.
Please visit www.21stcenturyskills.org for more information.

# TABLE OF CONTENTS

## CHAPTER ONE

# WHY PLANTS ARE IMPORTANT

*Plants that bear fruit provide food for humans and other animals.*

There could be no life on earth without plants. Plants are the only living things that can make energy from the sun. Every other living thing has to eat to get energy. Humans and other animals depend on plants for much of their food.

Plants come in all shapes and sizes. Different

parts of plants are used as food. Beets and carrots

are the roots of plants. Apples and bananas are the

fruits of plants. We eat stems of asparagus and leaves

of lettuce. The seeds of corn and rice plants

are the main foods in many countries.

Like humans, animals depend on plants

for food. Koalas eat the leaves of one type of

tree. Deer eat lots of different plants. Horses

eat grass and other plants. Even when animals

eat meat they are eating animals that ate plants.

When people eat chicken, bacon, and steaks,

they are eating food that came from plant-eating

21st Century Content

Today's cars are not just fueled by gasoline. Ethanol, made from plants, also fuels modern cars. In the United States ethanol is made mainly from corn. In Brazil it is made from sugarcane. Scientists are working to find ways to make ethanol from other plants. Among these are weeds and grasses and peelings from potatoes. Ethanol can be used in cars, outboard motors, lawnmowers, chain saws, snowmobiles, and other small engines.

*A fuzzy caterpillar finds food and shelter among the leaves of plants.*

animals. Milk and eggs come from cows and chickens that are

plant-eating animals.

Plants provide homes and shelter for many animals. Birds build nests in

trees. Caterpillars make their homes in plants. Timid salamanders hide under

fallen logs. During storms and harsh weather animals take shelter under plants.

Plants provide humans with material for shelter and clothing. Wood

to build our homes comes from trees. So does the wood for our tables and chairs. Cotton and linen to make our clothes comes from the fibers

of plants. So do the dyes that make them colorful. Wool for sweaters

comes from plant-eating animals. Silk comes from silkworms that feed

on leaves from mulberry trees.

Plants furnish raw materials for making many products. Ropes that

tie huge ships to docks are made from thousands of tiny plant fibers.

Roses, lilacs, and other flowers are used to make perfumes. Wood pulp

is used to make paper. Plants are also an important source of fuel. Some

*Plants provide raw materials for many things, including*
*the ropes that tie these boats to the dock.*

people burn wood to heat their homes and cook their food. People who

use coal, oil, and natural gas are using products from plants that lived long

ago. Coal began forming millions of years ago from dead plants. Oil and

natural gas were formed by decaying plants and animals in ancient oceans.

## REAL WORLD SCIENCE CHALLENGE

Plants take in **carbon dioxide** from the air. What happens to plants
when they cannot get air that brings them carbon dioxide? To find out,
cover the leaves of a plant with Vaseline, honey, or olive oil. Now air
is not able to get through to the tiny openings (pores) in the leaves.
Observe how the plant looks after a few days without carbon dioxide.
Wipe the covering from the leaves. What happens to the plant now?

*(Turn to page 29 for the answer)*

Plants have always been used to make medicines. Digitalis is a strong

heart medicine. It comes from the leaves of the foxglove plant. Quinine is

another example of an important medicinal plant. It is made from the bark of certain trees. Quinine is used to treat malaria, a disease that causes a flu-like illness that can be deadly.

Today scientists are studying many different plants. They hope to find chemicals in the plants that can be used to treat or cure cancer and other diseases.

Scientists who study plants are called botanists. So far, botanists have discovered and named over 375,000 kinds of plants. They discover more every day. Some plants are so tiny you need a microscope to see them. Others are so tall, you can hardly see their tops. Because plants are so important we need to understand how they grow and survive.

The study of plants can lead to many careers. Some botanists, or plant biologists, study the role of plants in the environment. Some search for new types of plants. Some try to find ways of using plants for medicines. Some study the structure of plants. Some work with farmers to help them grow stronger, healthier crops for people to eat. These are just some of the possible careers open to people who study and work with plants. As one botanist says, "As with any career, success depends on your productivity, and productivity follows hard work. But if you love what you do and are driven by it the hard work is fun work. I cannot imagine any other career being this much fun or rewarding."

## CHAPTER TWO

# HOW PLANTS GROW

In order to grow, plants need sunlight, air, water, and minerals.

Plants make their own food. To do this they need sunlight, air, water, and minerals. Plants' roots absorb water and minerals from the soil. Plants' leaves absorb sunlight.

Most plants grow from seeds. This is true for giant redwood trees and for tiny violets. Seeds come in different sizes and shapes and colors.

All seeds grow into the same kind of plant that made them. A sunflower seed grows into a sunflower. A seed from an oak tree grows into an oak tree.

A bean plant is an example of a plant that begins as a seed. The bean seed contains a tiny baby plant. This baby plant is called an embryo. The seed contains a supply of food for the embryo to use. A seed coat on the outside of the seed protects it. The seed absorbs water until its coat cracks. When this happens the seed breaks open. Then roots grow down and stems shoot up. Leaves begin to grow on the stems. The roots take in minerals and water. The stems carry the minerals and water to the leaves.

## REAL WORLD SCIENCE CHALLENGE

How does water get from the roots of a plant to its leaves high above the ground? To find out, put a stalk of celery in a glass of colored water. Watch what happens after a few hours. The next day cut across the stalk with a scissors. What do you see?

*(Turn to page 29 for the answer)*

*Like other plants, a pea plant makes its own food through photosynthesis.*

Then photosynthesis takes place. Photosynthesis is the scientific word for how plants make food. The leaves of the plant take in carbon dioxide from the air. The carbon dioxide enters the leaves through tiny holes, or pores. The leaves contain a green coloring called chlorophyll. Chlorophyll absorbs energy from sunlight. Plants use the sunlight, water, minerals, and carbon dioxide to make their food and release oxygen. The food the plants make is a simple sugar called glucose.

Glucose provides fuel for plants to live on.

Photosynthesis requires sunlight. So it cannot occur at night. During the hours of darkness, the plant releases its excess oxygen. The oxygen goes into the air that humans and other animals breathe and helps sustain life.

Some plants live in poor soil. They cannot get enough nutrients from it to make food. But they have found other ways to get the food they need. The Venus flytrap is an example of a meat-eating plant. It gives off a sweet juice called nectar. An insect smells the nectar. The insect crawls on a leaf of the Venus flytrap to taste the nectar. It touches the tiny hairs on the leaf. The

*The Venus flytrap, shown here, catches insects to get the minerals it needs.*

sides of the leaf slam shut. The insect is caught and cannot escape. Special

juices in the flytrap's leaves digest, or break down, the insect's body. The

Venus flytrap uses the minerals in the insect's body in making its food.

## REAL WORLD SCIENCE CHALLENGE

Roll up a sheet of dark-colored construction paper and put it in a clean glass jar. (The dark color is so your plant will show up well.) Fill the jar with water. Wedge a few bean seeds between the paper and the glass. Put the jar in a warm spot. Wait a few days. When the seeds sprout roots and shoots, place them in individual clay pots filled with soil. Place some of them in sunny spots. Put others in more shady spots. Put some in deep shade. Compare their rate of growth. Can you explain what happened?

(Turn to page 29 for the answer)

When the weather is dry, plants may have trouble getting water.

The colorful paintbrush plant has found a way to steal from other

plants. Paintbrushes often grow next to bluebonnets, a type of flower.

In dry spells the paintbrush's roots tap into the roots of the bluebonnet

*Giant redwood trees can live for thousands of years.*

plant next to it. It steals the bluebonnet's water and minerals. The

thirsty bluebonnet is left to wilt or die. If bluebonnets are not handy,

the paintbrush can get water from grass or even oak trees.

Some plants live a very long time. Others have very short lives.

Giant redwood trees in California live to be thousands of years old.

Others plants, like poppies, live for a season and then die.

## CHAPTER THREE

# HOW PLANTS REPRODUCE

*Bees help plants reproduce by spreading pollen from plant to plant.*

People find flowering plants pleasing. But plants do not have flowers

just to please people. The flowers are there for pollination. This is the

first step in making new plants. This process is called reproduction.

The stamen is the male part of a flower. It produces pollen. Pollen

looks like fine dust. The pistil is the female part of the flower.

In the pistil are unfertilized seeds called ovules.

Pollination happens when pollen from one flower's stamen reaches the ovules in another flower's pistil.

Since plants cannot move around, they need help with pollination. They use color, scent, and nectar to attract helpers. Bees are the most common helpers. Butterflies and hummingbirds also do this work. Other insects and animals also help out. While these visitors feed on the flower's nectar, pollen sticks to their bodies and legs. When they visit the next flower some of the pollen rubs off. If it reaches the ovules,

Orchids have ways to trick insects into pollinating them.

One kind of orchid looks like an insect that wasps hunt for food. The wasp dives at the orchid to sting it. And it leaves with a load of pollen glued to its body. It then carries the pollen to the next orchid it tries to sting. Some orchids have pouches under their lips. When a bee lands on the lip in search of nectar, it tumbles down into the pouch. The only way it can escape is by squeezing through a narrow passage lined with pollen. Orchids pollinated by moths are usually glistening white. They show up in the dark. And they give off their scents only at night. Some tropical orchids have a bad smell like decaying meat. Their odor attracts flies as pollinators.

*A ladybug visits a dandelion, one of the few flowering plants that can pollinate itself.*

pollination is complete. The ovule is fertilized. It then becomes a seed.

A new plant can grow from that seed.

Most flowering plants need help with pollination. But some can

manage on their own. The dandelion is one of these. The dandelion

can pollinate itself. Some violets also have a backup system. Most

of the time their open flowers attract visitors. But some of the violet's

flowers do not open. These flowers can fertilize themselves. Wheat

and other small grain plants are like this. These plants do not need brightly colored flowers. They do not need a scent to attract visitors.

And they do not need large amounts of pollen.

Pollination also occurs with the help of the wind. Much of the pollen

released into the air is wasted. So plants that depend on the wind produce

huge amounts of pollen. Corn is a wind-pollinated plant. Many grasses

and weeds, including ragweed, also use the wind for pollination.

After a plant is pollinated, its seeds mature. Then they need to find a place

to grow. Sometimes birds or other animals swallow the seeds when they eat

*Seeds attached to the light, fluffy down of the milkweed plant are carried by the wind.*

the fruit. Then the seeds are deposited in the droppings of the animals. Some

seeds are covered with burrs. These often hitchhike on animal fur or human

clothing. The seeds of milkweed are carried by the wind on silky parachutes.

Coconut seeds are sometimes carried a long way by water to new homes.

Other seeds such as acorns and pecans are buried in new places by squirrels.

## REAL WORLD SCIENCE CHALLENGE

How do roots grow? Use a carrot to find out how roots grow. Cut off the bottom third of a fresh carrot. Stick three toothpicks in the carrot to form a ring around the carrot. Place the carrot in a jar or glass half full of water. Use the toothpicks to hold the carrot up on the rim of the glass or jar. Let the bottom of the carrot touch the water. Put it in a sunny spot. What happens after a few days?

(Turn to page 29 for the answer)

Most plants grow from seeds. But some plants have more than one

way of reproducing. Strawberry plants have runners that spread out over

the ground. A part of the runner with small leaves is called a node. New

*Strawberry plant runners take root once they touch the ground.*

strawberry plants appear where the nodes touch the ground and grow

roots. Some grasses send out underground runners that grow new plants.

Plants like daffodils reproduce from bulbs. In warm weather new bulbs

appear on the side of the parent bulb. The baby bulbs grow into new

plants in the spring. Ferns do not make pollen or seeds. They drop tiny

cells called spores to make new plants.

Plants have many ways of reproducing. They also have many ways

of surviving in difficult situations.

## CHAPTER FOUR

# How Plants Survive

*The giant saguaro cactus collects water through shallow roots
and then stores it for use during the dry days ahead.*

Plants are found all over the world except in places that are always

covered with ice. Even under harsh conditions plants have found ways

to adapt so they can survive.

No plant can live without water. In hot, dry places plants called cacti (the plural of cactus) thrive. Plants lose water through their leaves. Long ago cacti stopped growing leaves like other plants. Cacti have their own ways of saving each drop of water. Giant saguaros have shallow roots. These roots reach in every direction. When rain does come, the shallow roots collect it. Other cacti, like prickly pears, store water in thick, waxy stems. The night-blooming cereus stores water in a huge root that looks like a big turnip.

Some plants and insects survive by helping each other. The yucca plant and a small moth are one example of this. When yucca flowers open, the moth gathers pollen. It rolls the pollen into a ball. Then it carries it to another yucca plant. It stuffs the pollen ball into the female part of the flower. This pollinates the yucca. The yucca then can make its seeds. The moth lays an egg in a pollinated yucca flower. The egg hatches into a caterpillar. It lives in the yucca seedpod. The caterpillar feeds on some of the yucca seeds. When the caterpillar is ready to form a cocoon, it chews a hole in the yucca seedpod. It crawls out and spins a thread. Using the thread, it lowers itself to the ground. It burrows a few inches into the soil. It spins a silken cocoon around itself. There it remains snug in its cocoon during the winter. The following spring it emerges as an adult moth—just as the yucca is in bloom. And the cycle begins again.

*Tiny hairs on the stems of the Arctic poppy protect it
from the bitter cold of its environment.*

On the tops of mountains, chilly winds make life hard for plants.

Trees have adapted by growing small. Other plants in high places hug

the ground. Arctic poppies have a blanket of tiny hairs. These hairs hold

in heat. In New Zealand, the mountain crowfoot grows on snowy Mount

Cook. This tiny plant survives the icy cold by making a substance that

keeps water from freezing.

Most plants do not like saltwater. They need freshwater to grow.

Plants that grow by the sea have adapted. Mangrove trees are found along tropical shorelines. They grow in shallow water. They take in seawater and release the salt through special leaf openings. Or they send the salt to dying leaves. When the dead leaves drop off, the salt goes with them. Some hardy saltwater plants have large, swollen leaves. They use these leaves to store rainwater.

*Unlike most other plants, mangrove trees thrive in salty water.*

## REAL WORLD SCIENCE CHALLENGE

Take a walk in your neighborhood or in a park in the spring and in the fall. Look at the trees. How do they look in the spring? Write down your observations. What is different about some of them in the fall? Have the leaves on a tree turned different colors? Write down your observations again. Compare your observations from spring and fall. Can you explain what happened?

*(Turn to page 29 for the answer)*

In tropical rain forests leaves of tall trees form a thick cover. The floor of the forest is always in deep shade. But ferns and other shade-loving plants make themselves at home under the towering trees. Thick vines wind up the trees to reach the sunlight. Tropical orchids grow high up on the trees.

Unlike animals, plants cannot run away from their enemies. They have to protect themselves in other ways. They have developed special weapons for this purpose. Creatures that feed on plants range from tiny insects to large animals. Small insects suck the plant's sap or chew on its leaves. Large animals may eat the entire plant.

Cacti have strong defenses. Some have swordlike leaves with barbed edges. Others depend on spines and thorns. Beautiful roses attract flying pollinators. But the sharp thorns of roses protect them from plant-eating animals. Thistles have prickles that jab intruders' tender mouths.

Other plants have other ways to protect themselves. Some of them taste awful. Once an animal tastes them, it leaves the plant alone. Grazing cattle never disturb the creosote bush. It

**21st Century Content**

There are many ways in which the activities of people endanger plants.

People cut down trees to make wood and paper products. Trees are also cut down to make space for farms and houses. Ocean floors are drilled for oil. Leaks or spills from oil rigs and tankers kill plants on which animals feed. When wetlands are drained, water plants die. Pesticides and pollution from factories also kill plants.

Some plants are in danger because they are so attractive. One example is the bluebell. It looks like a beautiful blue bouquet. But when it is pulled up by the roots, it cannot reproduce. The same thing happens when collectors dig up unusual cacti to put in their gardens.

*The yucca plant's sharp, pointed leaves provide protection from predators.*

has nasty-tasting oil-filled leaves. Stinging nettles have needlelike hairs. When an animal brushes against them they puncture its skin. The nettles release a mixture of juices. These juices cause a stinging pain. Since the animal does not want another unpleasant shot, it will leave the nettle alone.

Over millions of years plants have adapted in order to survive. We are lucky they adapted and survived because *we* depend on *them* to survive!

# REAL WORLD SCIENCE CHALLENGE ANSWERS

## Chapter One
Page 8

The leaves you covered will look sickly and yellowish. They could get sunlight. But they could not get air to bring them carbon dioxide. When you uncover the leaves they may become healthy. But if they were covered too long, they will die and drop off.

## Chapter Two
Page 11

Plants need sunlight to make their food. That's why food making is done in the daytime.

Look at the differences in the size of your plants. You will see the ones that got the most sunlight are the largest and healthiest.

Page 14

Plants do not have hearts to pump water and nutrients through them. But they do have a way to get water and food to the parts that need them. Inside plants are passages or tubes for water and minerals to travel through. When a tube joins a wet and a dry place, water is drawn toward the dry place. After a few hours the leaves in your colored water will begin to turn the color of the water.

When you cut the celery you expose the tubes. You will see how the water was drawn up into them. You will also see how it traveled up the tubes to reach the leaves.

## Chapter Three
Page 20

Carrots store food in their roots. When you supply the carrot root with water and sunlight it uses the energy stored in its root to sprout. Then it grows into a new tall, leafy carrot plant.

## Chapter Four
Page 26

The trees that have dropped their leaves are *deciduous* (leaf-losing).

During the short days of the winter months, there is less sunlight for photosynthesis.

When the weather turns cooler, the chlorophyll in the leaves begins to break down.

As the chlorophyll disappears, the leaf color changes. Its true color is red, yellow, brown, or orange. This is what shows when the chlorophyll is gone. Then the leaf dies and falls to the ground. The tree is adapting to the cold weather.

It will use the energy it has stored to survive until spring and longer, warmer days return.

# GLOSSARY

carbon dioxide (karbun die OX ide) the gas animals breathe out, which green plants use to make food

chlorophyll (CLOR o fil) green pigment in plants that absorbs energy from sunlight

embryo (EM brio) the part of a seed that develops into a new plant

node (node) position on plant stem from which new leaves, shoots, and roots grow

nutrients (NEW tree ents) substances needed to sustain life

ovules (AH vulz) parts of the plant that develop into seeds when fertilized

oxygen (OX i jen) gas that humans and animals must breathe to stay alive, which green plants release into the air while making food

photosynthesis (foto SIN the sis) process by which plants, using the energy of sunlight, produce sugars from carbon dioxide, water, and minerals

pistil (PISS tul) ovule-bearing, female part of a flowering plant

pollination (paul i NAE shun) transfer of male pollen to the female pistil, usually with the help of pollinators such as insects, birds, or wind

stamen (STAY men) male part of a flower that produces pollen

# FOR MORE INFORMATION

## Books

Burnie, Davie. *Plant*. Eyewitness Books Series. New York: DK, 2004.

Halfmann, Janet. *Plant Tricksters*. New York: Scholastic Library, 2004.

Hopkins, William G., ed. *Plant Development*. Green World Series. Philadelphia: Chelsea House, 2006.

Llewellyn, Claire. *Understanding Plants*. New York: Black Rabbit Books, 2007.

## Web Sites

### Desert Plants and Wildflowers
*http://www.desertusa.com/flora.html*
Detailed information on how desert plants survive heat and dryness

### The Great Plant Escape
*http://www.urbanext.uiuc.edu/*
A fun way to learn plant structure and behavior. Spanish option available

### Noteworthy Plants
*http://waynesword.palomar.edu/index*
Descriptions of interesting plants. Many links to articles about individual plants

### Plants and Our Environment
*http://library.thinkquest.org*
More information on pollination, photosynthesis, and seed reproduction

# INDEX

## ABOUT THE AUTHOR

Elizabeth Silverthorne has written more than twenty books for adults and children. Her book *Legends and Lore of Texas Wildflowers* was published by Texas A&M University Press. She especially enjoys writing biographies and books and articles about history. Her hobbies are reading and traveling. She lives in the village of Salado in the heart of Texas.